The Loss

of

A Child

Motivator

Mikkita L. Moore

The Loss of A Child

The Loss of A Child

ISBN: 979-8-9884628-1-1
Imprint: Invisible Daughter, LLC

Printed and bounded in the United States of America.

The Loss of A Child

<u>Thank You</u>

The Loss of A Child

The Loss of A Child

Special Thanks & Dedication

Thank all of you for making this book possible!

All the Authors: *Mikkita Moore, Dana Owens, Lisa Seymour, Madam Jai Qui, Timothia Reid*

Graphic Designer: *Shawn Robinson, of 727 Marketing... It's been a pleasure to work with you!!*

Editor: *Invisible Daughter, LLC team.... Thank you for your dedication to making sure the company runs smoothly.*

This book is dedicated to all those that have survived The Loss of A Child

This one is for you!

The Loss of A Child

Table of Contents

The Loss of A Child

The Loss of A Child

The Loss of A Child

Chapter One

The Loss is not Always Just Death

Mikkita L Moore

Mikkita L Moore, an author, Realtor, international motivational speaker and mother of five, starting at the tender age of 14 from the South Side of Chicago. Mikkita is the Founder and CEO of *The Art of Transparency, NFP* an organization with a vision and mission to "Heal ONE Person, One City, ONE State, ONE Nation at a time. We provide the pivotal tools resources and fundamental needs necessary to create lasting impact for those affected by various traumas.". The CEO of *Invisible Daughter, LLC* a publishing and Writing Coach Company. Although passionate about teaching others about her journey which includes forgiving a father that wasn't, in her opinion, able to be the model man she had desperately needed as a young girl growing into womanhood, she continued to struggle with her inner feelings. Being able to convey these imbedded emotions is also comforting for her. Learning the *Art of Transparency* is equivalent to facing and being fully aware of who she is, her ability to candidly speak from the heart about real life issues and how to conquer life's trials is one of my greatest gifts.

Speaking to participants is a time for meaningful engagement. Speaking to encourage, lead and offer real life situations and results to enable listeners to truly understand and connect with her, not only as the speaker but to have empathy for the topic. One of the results that Mikkita obtains when speaking to audiences is her dynamic ability to ignite an awakening within those who hear her story. It allows them to realize and understand their issue more clearly, that she has been through similar situations and how they, too, can overcome the feelings and possible stagnation from its impact. These processes are all facilitated with the audience in mind.

How beneficial it is to have the skill to ignite the path of change. Mikkita's niche is engaging her audience with realistic topics that help identify the issues and the willingness to work towards resolutions. Her first two books, *The Letter From, the Invisible Daughter* as well as *The Cause and Effect of The Invisible Daughter*, talk about, among other topics, parenting a child that's different from the rest and her doubts of being a good mother. As she speaks candidly about her thoughts of suicide and being in unsafe relationships that included domestic violence; emotional, mental and physical, she creates and implements strategies to be used in the moment to begin healing processes for others. Most gatherings include hands-on activities. There's only room for results; a growth mindset. Mikkita continues to receive multiple invites to speak due this direct approach which call for peace and progress in the lives of others.

During the pandemic of 2020, Mikkita was blessed to birth another seven books through collaborations with other Authors, giving her a total of nine published books. In the words of Mikkita about what inspired her to write her books... *With all of my books I wanted to reach my audience on a level that's different from the rest. I needed to reach an audience that hasn't heard about the Black girl from the south side of Chicago that wasn't poor and not knowing where her next meal would come from. The girl that her mother wasn't a drug addict, father wasn't a drug pusher. I was tired of the stereotypes that I had to be from this type of family or that kind of family because I had my first child at the age of 14 years old. My all-time favorite was the one that says teenage moms can't raise their children effectively or the one that says teenage moms are all high school dropouts. Neither of which proves true for me.*

My books are not about the average poor Black girl living in poverty. My book is about my life, from the perspective of a teenage mom that didn't struggle, that didn't drop out of high school but in fact graduated high school a year ahead of time with honors. This book is my life from a perspective that thought about suicide, went through domestic violence, emotionally mentally and physically. This book talks from a perspective of not feeling the love of my father searching for that type of love from boys/men that either couldn't give it or just didn't know how to give love.

My books talk about parenting a child that's different from the rest of her five children. Wondering where I went wrong as a parent, or as a real mother. I talk about being fatherless and how that affects my relationships with men. In my books I talk about how my struggle with alcohol was the only way I could cope with the depression and anger that was built from all the "life issues" that I didn't know how to let go of. My books come from real life situations that happens in our community far too often and overlooked because it's not society's "norm".

Mikkita along with The Art of Transparency, NFP tour has scheduled and appeared for several presentations and speaking engagements, over the last five years with heightened interest in each state. Moving forward there will be plans to host expos, workshops and conferences on trauma healing and awareness. This tour has touched over 1 million lives through the AOT tour platform, the AOT TV and Talk show, as well as their community outreach.

www.mikkitamoore.com
info@mikkitamoore.com

www.artoftransparency.org
info@artoftransparency.org

The Loss is Not Always Just Death

It is so crazy that I never thought I would be writing about this subject…. The Loss of my child….. Wow…

Well, I guess I need to start with… I didn't even know that the child was there for real…

September maybe October of 2010 I found out that I was pregnant, now this pregnancy came as a complete shock because for four maybe five years prior to this I was told that I could not have any more children. I was diagnosed with fibroid tumors on both my tubes. I was told that if those cysts ever burst, I would be in extreme pain as well as have severe bleeding. Well, none of that occurred.

I remember running into my ex in a mall after not seeing him in years, him saying, "*hey isn't your birthday next week*", me saying, "*yep*", and him saying, "*let's get together and go out*"…. No big deal it's just sex, right? Ha!!! Wrong… That one night changed my life forever!

Before running into my daughter's father (my ex), I was dating a guy for three and a half years and didn't even have a pregnancy scare let alone being pregnant, therefore I just knew that I was not ever going to be pregnant again.

The week of my birthday which is September 18th, I hung out with the ex, and we did what grown people tend to do…. After that night, I didn't talk to him nor did I want to, it was fun but nothing more than that. Now, don't ask me

20

what made me take a pregnancy test because I really don't know, I just know that four weeks later, I wasn't feeling right, I was feeling really sluggish, lazy and just all around weird. I remember going to Walgreen's and getting the cheapest test on the shelf. I came home took the test and it immediately showed two lines… I instantly said… "No way, this can not be right". I went back to the store and got one of each test on that same shelf, I think it had to have been maybe six different tests. Got home, took all six tests, and they were all POSITIVE again. I thought to myself, wait a minute how the heck did this happen... and furthermore who's baby is this?

No for real, I said exactly that, you have to understand, I had a part-time boyfriend at this time, and I had been with my ex that one night. The boyfriend and I had been together three and a half years with no baby, so we didn't use any type of birth control, and my ex and I, well I don't know what that was about, but we used nothing to protect ourselves either. Lord if being young and dumb was a person….

Shortly after taking the pregnancy tests, I made my doctor's appointment for the next day. The doctor confirmed what I already knew... Mikkita you my dear are indeed pregnant. I went for ultrasound maybe a week later, at the ultrasound, I measured six to eight weeks, being told to schedule another ultrasound with a high-risk doctor because they could still see the cyst on one of my ovaries. I made the appointment, had the second ultrasound and everything was going great, until…..

The Loss of A Child

One night a few months into my pregnancy, while with my Forbidden Fruit, (a story that you will have to read in the book titled "The Soul Tie of The Forbidden Fruit") doing what grown people do, I started to bleed extremely heavy, I was rushed to the hospital to learn that I was having a miscarriage and there was nothing that they could medically do to stop the process. They sent me home and told me what to look for during this miscarriage and when to come back to the hospital to get any medical procedures that I would need following the passing of the miscarried fetus.

For the next few days, I was in pain but not really bleeding much. At the end of the third day, I started to bleed heavily and decided to go back to the ER. When I got to the ER, the nurse took me straight to the back, during the exam my baby passed through. My baby was so very tiny, no real featured but she had eyes and a heartbeat. I saw her heartbeat for an entire minute which seemed like forever. A few hours later I was sent home, to heal, but something still just did not feel right.

Two days after the miscarriage, I returned to the doctor for what we thought would be a D and C procedure (Dilation and Curettage is a procedure to remove tissue from inside your uterus), however, to our shock there was a hidden baby. All this time I was pregnant with fraternal twins, and no one knew.

When I arrived at the doctor for the procedure, I was immediately sent to ultrasound to be sure everything had passed through, the first ultrasound technician shockingly asked, "Ms. Moore, are you here for an after-miscarriage ultrasound?", I responded, "unfortunately, yes, I am." She then said, "hold on a second, let me get a senior tech to look at this, I'll be right back." Me laying there confused, I mean I had never had a miscarriage before so I wasn't sure if I should be worried or if this was the regular thing to hear. When she returned maybe fifteen minutes later, she was accompanied by the Senior Lab Tech, my Doctor, and another OB/GYN. All of which was watching the screen as she rolled the ultrasound wand around my stomach. All of a sudden, one of the Doctors hollered "STOP! That's a heartbeat right there, go back." The whole room got quiet and sure enough, there was a heartbeat. My baby's heartbeat was in rhythm with mine, so we didn't hear it. Strange right, yeah that's what we ALL said.

That's when I knew this baby was going to be real special. She survived a partial miscarriage, and nobody knew she was even there.

I was sent home on bedrest, the doctor told me no walking unless it was to the bathroom and back to bed, making sure I kept my feet elevated at least twelve hours a day. I had never had a miscarriage before, I have never had any real complications in regard to a pregnancy. I had been pregnant four times prior to this, and I had four live births. My youngest son, the child right before my baby girl was premature by six weeks, but the doctors said that was from climbing to the fourth floor several times a day and standing on my feet while doing hair all day, every day. My son had no complications after birth, he was in the NICU for about seven days and was released to come home. So having a miscarriage, a partial miscarriage at that was very new to me.

After having a partial miscarriage and finding out that I was pregnant with two girls, I just didn't know how to feel, I wondered what she would be like, would she look like me or would she be an identical look of her sister. I often wondered if the second baby would have been a surprise at birth or would we have found her later in the pregnancy. There were so many questions, there were so many mixed feelings. I missed something I never truly knew was there.

My surviving daughter was born June 10th, 2011 at 37 weeks, a healthy six pounds one once bouncing baby. She was so little, yet so smart. When she was two years old, she would have tea parties with her angel sister, I know for some this sounds crazy but for me, I knew her imaginary friend was actually her angel sister. My baby girl has been an angel right here on earth. She saved my life in 2013 from suicide attempt, she saved my mother's life when she wanted to give up after being diagnosed with breast cancer in 2010, and colon cancer in 2016. I am not sure if she and her angel sister get together to have a meeting about what's going on down here on earth, but I do know that my angel baby is still right here, watching over us and making sure that we are good.

Surviving a loss is not easy at all, and sometimes the loss is not just death. In 2011, the same year my daughter was born, I began to lose my middle son to the streets. No, not loose as in death but loss as in the streets became part of who he was, and I couldn't save him. I tried everything, including packing my entire life up and moving to St. Louis, MO in 2014. From 2011 until 2014 my son ran away, was arrested countless times and placed in foster care, becoming a ward of the state. To save him I decided that it would be best to move away and start fresh, well I was a little too late, in July of 2014 my son was arrested for firearm possession (he was only 15 years old) he was facing a sentence of ten years. I felt like my world had come to an end. I blamed myself, I was hurt, I was angry. From 2014 until 2016 he was in juvenile detention, being released in August of 2016. He came home and was a scholar student and a great son….. UNTIL…..

I started getting phone calls from the school stating that he had been missing classes, not turning in assignments and would walk out of the school at random. At that very moment I knew I was once again losing him to the streets, but this time, we were living in St, Louis with no one I could call to make sure he was at least safe out there. He would come in all times of the night, he started arguing with me again, becoming a menace to society all over again. On May 18th, 2017, my son turned 18, and by this time I was tired, my mom's health was okay but not its best, my oldest daughter was pregnant with her first child, and I was over trying to save him from not only the streets but from himself, I decided that I would move home (back to Chicago). May 24th, 2017, I packed a moving truck with all my belongings and headed home. I had given my son the option of moving back with me, but he said that he was grown and didn't need to be smothered by his mother, he stated that he would be fine on his own, I said a prayer, turned off the lights, closed the door and walked away.

By the end of July of that same year, at 4am, I received "THE" call… "*Ma, they got me and I am going to be here for a while!*, he said… "*Son, what happened, what do you mean*", I responded, "*Ma, stop crying, because now at least you know where I am*", he said… My son has been in jail since then, I have not laid eyes on him since November of 2017, when I went to see him in the county jail of St. Louis. He was sentenced to ten years in 2018, having to do at least 60% of his sentence.

Yes, I talk to him, but the hole in my heart is big, and it has felt like a loss for now over ten years. My prayer is that when they release him this time, I can get my SON back, he is not a baby anymore (24 years old to be exact), but he will always be my baby.

Lord, please change his heart, change his mindset, when they let him go THIS time, let him be the man that I know I raised him to be, let him be the man society can honor, and I can be proud of. Let him be a man of his word and of high integrity... Please father I ask of this in your name… Amen!

I know this one is a completely different type of loss, and in hopes, I can get this loss back, but my heart at this point doesn't really know the difference, all my heart knows is, I have an angel in heaven and a son that my heart can't reach. It all hurts the same for me.

To the person that reads this book, say a prayer for us, we all are still fighting this battel day by day, minute by minute, sometimes second by second… For those that have suffered the loss of a child know that you are not alone. We are all in this together, it may not feel like it right now, but your heart will ease, and days will get lighter, hold on to God's unchanging hand to see us all through.

Until next time…..

The Loss of A Child

Chapter Two

Faith of A Mustard Seed

Dana Owens

Meet **Dana Owens**, a Chicago-based woman who has a passion for crafting, fashion, and food. Her love for these activities has led her to become a great connector of women who share the same interests. Dana is a firm believer in women supporting women and she has made it her mission to uplift, encourage, and motivate them to reach their full potential.

Dana's greatest accomplishment in life so far is becoming a mother. Her experience in motherhood has led her to help other women through their own motherhood journeys. She understands the challenges that come with motherhood and is always willing to lend a listening ear or a helping hand to other women who may need it.

Looking into the future, Dana hopes to build a community of women who can come together in a safe space to share resources and ideas that will help enhance their quality of life. She envisions a community where women can connect, grow, and thrive together. With her passion for bringing women together and her dedication to helping them succeed, Dana is sure to make her dream a reality.

Faith of A Mustard Seed

Do not speak anything into or over your life that you do not want to become a reality.

About 1 in 4 pregnancies end in miscarriage. I am a part of the 1 in 4 community.

Miscarriage and stillbirth are intense and unique forms of trauma that often results with women suffering in silence. Following a miscarriage comes the feeling of anxiety, depression, grief, guilt, shame, and stress. Experiencing a miscarriage can have many negative effects on your mental health. Often after going through this traumatic experience women are expected to just go on with their lives as if nothing happened. What some people don't understand is, it's something that you never forget but learn how to move forward. Studies have proven even after the birth of a healthy child; the mother still experiences sadness and depression from the previous loss of a child. A part of you always wonders what things would be like had you not experienced this loss.

Most women blame themselves for having a miscarriage when it's not their fault. On top of the effects on your mental health miscarriage can also affect your physical health. Women who have reoccurring miscarriages are more likely to develop blood clots and heart disease.

Within the African American community there are some things that people do not talk about, Family secrets, miscarriages, and infertility. Black women are less likely to seek medical assistance for infertility mainly due to embarrassment, and lack of knowledge. There are so many negative connotations surrounding infertility within our community. Also, there's a huge misconception that infertility does not exist in the black community.

I speak up and I speak out. I share my experience with family, friends, associates, as well as complete strangers. I was chosen for this. I was called to this experience, so, that I can help others along the way, who look like me and think they are all alone. I was appointed and anointed to tackle this journey, I have the strength to inspire, encourage, and support other women. In the words of Sara Jakes Roberts all it takes is one woman. One woman to break generational curses. One woman to speak up and out. One woman to share her story. One woman to change the narrative. One woman to build community and a support system for other women. One woman to provide information and resources. God decided to Bless me with this assignment. In the beginning, I used to wonder why me, but now I feel privileged that it *IS* me. It's an honor and privilege to know my story is bringing awareness to something so personal and often so forgotten. It's an honor and privilege to know that women younger, older, as well as the same age as I, trust me with something so personal to support them through it.

For years I suffered in silence, blamed myself and questioned my faith, until one day my perspective of this journey completely changed. In the beginning, I never expressed to others what I was going through or how it made me feel. I am the true example of not looking like what I have been through.

The Loss of A Child

Here's my story of being young and having the faith of a mustard seed while quietly battling infertility. As referenced earlier, be careful of the words you speak. There is power in the tongue and as you read more you will understand why I say that.

In my early 20s, I wasn't really thinking about becoming a mom. I was enjoying life, building my clientele, and establishing my career as a hairstylist. One year, at Thanksgiving dinner, my dad asked me when I was going to give him a grandchild. I told him that's not something on my mind right now, I have time. He told me not to wait too long or I will have trouble after a certain age. I laughed it right off and said if I run into trouble, I will just go to a fertility specialist and do IVF (in vitro fertilization).

Now as I sat there and said that I did not think it would become my reality. It's not something I was opposed to be doing, however I just never thought I would need to. I didn't know much about IVF back then I also didn't know anyone personally who had ever done it. As I reflect on my childhood and young adult years, I don't recall ever hearing a black woman talk about having a miscarriage or experiences with infertility. Not hearing about it, often made you think it was truly not something that black women went or go through. I knew some of what the IVF process consist of, and I knew it was something the rich people did. Again, I wasn't concerned about learning more because I was young, healthy, and fit. And did I mention becoming a mom was not on my mind at that time of my life.

The Loss of A Child

A few years later, I started dating a nice gentleman. As I got to know him more, I started to envision a future with him that included marriage and having children. The relationship grew and things became more serious between us.

For me my menstrual cycle would always come on time each month and last about 3 to 4 days. It was never ever late, always 28 days apart. Well one month, it did not arrive when it was supposed to. I took a pregnancy test and sure enough it was positive. I scheduled a doctor's appointment, went and of course the doctor confirmed the pregnancy.

Excitement was starting to build in me and of course he was excited. Almost as soon as the excitement started to build the joy was ripped away when I started to experience abdominal pain and bleeding. Went to the hospital, they told me the devasting news, I was having a miscarriage. There was no medical explanation provided as to why I was experiencing a miscarriage, but the Doctor assured me that I would be able to conceive again and have a baby. I cried for a day or two and returned to my normal routine like nothing happened. I never talked about this horrible experience and a lot of people that know me probably knew nothing about it. My body quickly returned to normal or what I thought was normal. My menstrual cycle was back to every 28days without interruption.

In the meantime, others around me are getting pregnant and having babies with no problem. Of course, you are happy for those that are blessed with the opportunity to become mothers, but at the same time you have this sadness still within you. At some point, I tricked myself into thinking I

34

was completely over the experience of that type of loss. I feel happy again. I feel relaxed and stress free. My monthly friend disappeared again. History repeats itself and at 9 weeks I had another miscarriage. After healing, I had tests done and was once again assured that I would be able to conceive and have a baby naturally.

My faith was being tested and I was starting to ask why me? Every time I saw the news and heard about a baby being abandoned, or worse, by their parents, it really broke my heart. Every time I saw someone with substance abuse issues pregnant it really bothered me. Why are they able to conceive, carry and give birth, when they are not deserving of it? It felt like I was slowly dying on the inside while I was suffering with grief and thought that I would never become a mom.

Now let's talk about the horrible comments and unsolicited advice that comes with being a black woman of a certain age with no children. One top of being a woman over a certain age, a black woman over a certain age, and add being a married woman to it. People would automatically assume that I had children based on my age. When I would tell them that I do not have any children, some people would ask me again as if I am lying. Comments from others would be, "girl you're that old and married and you don't have kids, something must be wrong with you. What are you waiting for, why don't you have kids, you are going to be old."

Several years have passed since my last miscarriage, I started to believe that I could not have a child. I was forcing myself to accept the fact that it was not going to be a mother, this truly became a reality for me. However, every time someone would mind my uterus, and ask me an insensitive question about not having a child, I had to cover my true feelings. I was so tired of making up stories and or saying I did not want to have kids. What I didn't realize is that, making up stories and saying things I did not really mean to answer questions about my reproductive system is that I was speaking against what I wanted. Truth be told, I did not have to respond to people asking me those questions. It's simply not their business so I should not have felt the need to answer them.

Some people don't mean any harm when asking "when are you going to have kids", but I have learned it's a question that you should not ask people. You never know what traumatic experiences a person has had before. You don't know if they are grieving from miscarriage, stillbirth, termination due to heath reasons, adoption that they might not have really wanted to do. Believe it or not there are some women who truly have no desire to have children and that is perfectly fine. It does not make you any more or any less of a woman because you do not have any children. Although, I can tell you from personal experience it makes you feel less of a woman when you want it and are having trouble accomplishing it.

Now, I'm in my late 20's, I started to notice that my cycle was weird. It arrived when it should have and in 2 days it was gone. About two weeks later, I started to bleed again for a couple more days. I called to schedule a doctor's appointment so that I can try to figure out what is going on. My appointment was two weeks away, during that time I felt perfectly fine. The day of my appointment arrived, I told my doctor what was going on and she said let's do a pregnancy test. I laughed saying taking a test would be a waste of time because I know I cannot get pregnant but go ahead, do the test. I provided the urine sample, she came back in the room, did the test right in front of me and said girl you're pregnant. I was completely surprised, that is not the news I was expecting. She estimated that I was around 9 weeks pregnant, she then ordered an early ultrasound due to my prior history. Well, I never made it to my ultrasound appointment.

I woke up one night out of my sleep with a sharp pain in my butt. I had never felt that pain before and then it just went away. I went back to sleep, the next day I went to work like nothing happened. At work that sharp pain came back, I thought maybe I was hungry, so, I went to get food. The pain started to happen more rapidly; I knew something was not right. I left work early, went home and called my husband. I told him that I needed to go to that hospital. While I was waiting for him to get home the pain increased, I could barely walk.

I was rushed to the hospital; they did what felt like a two-hour ultrasound. I was in so much pain it was horrible. During the ultrasound, I kept asking if the baby was okay, the tech just kept saying the Doctor will talk to you. They took me back to my room, the Doctor came in, informed me that the baby was growing in my tube which caused my tube to rupture, and that I was bleeding internally. I had to go into emergency surgery to get my tube removed, which ultimately terminated the pregnancy. The physical healing process afterwards was hard. I was in so much pain, I wanted nothing more than for this pain to go away.

Two months later, I went in for testing again, I am sure you already know what they told me. Everything looks fine, even though I only have one tube, I would still be able to get pregnant naturally with no problem. I've heard that one too many times before, so, at this point, I refuse to believe it.

I started doing research to find a fertility specialist to go to. I finally found a specialist who had great reviews, with many accolades and I scheduled an appointment with her. Prior to the appointment her staff requested my medical records so she would have them available to review. Also, I received a packet of paperwork from her office that I needed to fill out and bring into the appointment with me. I did not know what to expect from my initial appointment. The day of my appointment the only person in the office who looked like me was the receptionist. As I waited in the waiting room, other patients were coming in and out, none of them looked like me. Most of them were white women.

I eagerly sat there waiting for my name to be called. The nurse called me to the back, walking me to the doctor's office. I was so nervous as I waited for her to come in. She entered the room with a big smile on her face and extended her hand to shake mine. I sat back down; we go straight to business. She went over my medical records and the paperwork that I had to fill out from her office. Then she explained the initial process to getting things started. The first hurdle was for her office to contact my insurance company to get approval for service. After the approval, there will be a series of testing to see if any issues are discovered, then she will come up with a plan of action. I was so excited after my consultation with her, I have never met a doctor that made me feel relaxed, at peace, and in good hands. The more she talked and explained things to me, the more I felt a sense of peace and calmness over me.

About a week later, I received a letter from the insurance company denying approval for fertility services. According to the insurance company, since I was able to get pregnant on my own before, I do not need assistance from a specialist. I was so upset; I called the doctor's office, spoke with the nurse, she said she would have the Dr to call me. About an hour later the Dr called me and said not to worry she will deal with the insurance company. Clearly there is some type of issue if you are having reoccurring miscarriages. I don't know what she sent to or said to the insurance company, but I received a letter from the insurance company saying I am approved for services with the fertility specialist.

The receptionist called me to schedule my appointment to come in for blood work. When undergoing fertility treatment everything is based around your cycle. There were tons of blood test done to check different hormone levels. Ultrasounds were done to get my reproductive organs, HSG test and more. Finally done with testing, now it's time to meet the doctor again to go over the game plan. What she discovered is that my reproductive organs are completely healthy and capable of producing life.

However, what she discovered that the regular gynecologist missed is that one of my hormones was off. I started taking a pill to help with regulating my hormones and they tracked my ovulation to let me know the best time to have adult activities. Fourteen days after I would go in for a pregnancy test and it was negative.

When I was going through this experience there were so many emotions I was feeling. The hormones were controlling my body, I was emotional, I was tired, but I knew all of this was worth it. I started to open up to others about going to a fertility specialist, some people would tell me how wrong I was for going to a specialist, I was trying to play God, saying "if God wanted me to have a baby, he would have given me one". One top of not seeing anyone who looks like me when going to the Dr, receiving negative comments, and not having anyone to talk to who truly understands what I am going through. Even though I had all of this stacked against me or at least I felt like I had things stacked against me, it wasn't going to stop me from getting to my end goal…. *my baby*.

Met with my specialist again to go over the new plan. If plan "A" doesn't work, go to plan "B", but never change the end goal. She explained the process of doing IVF to conceive, she broke everything down so that I completely understood the process. I was ready for the task, my mindset shifted. If I was going to conceive and have a baby, I first had to believe that I was worthy of it.

I stopped doubting myself. I stopped hoping and wishing and instead I started praying, expressing gratitude. Every day during my IVF process I prayed. I prayed for the health of my womb. I thanked God for making my body healthy and strong enough to conceive and give birth to a baby. I thanked God for making me a mother.

The Loss of A Child

During IVF, you are supposed to take your meds for two-weeks, but my body took so well to the meds that I had so many eggs, I was able to stops my meds after only one week. Went in for surgery to have my eggs harvested and fertilized. A few weeks later, I went in and had two of my embryos transferred into my uterus. About a week later I took a blood test to see if I was pregnant, the Dr. is like it's early, normally we test at 14 days but let's just see. Test came back positive. My beta levels were rapidly increasing and were extremely high in a short period of time, which made the nurse believe I must be pregnant with twins.

My beta was high, but my ultrasound only showed one sac and one baby. I went in for my six-week checkup with ultrasound and received a big surprise, it showed two babies with two heartbeats in a shared sac. Wow identical twins, such an unexpected blessing. This was a rare pregnancy, and I was monitored very closely. The twins should have been in their own sac but instead they shared a sac.

Now, the issue is, as they grow, will there be enough blood supply to get to both of them to allow them to continue to develop. I had to go to the doctor every two days for blood work and ultrasound. Although the pregnancy was risky with a low chance of survival, things seemed to be going well. I had an appointment on a Friday, everything was fine, went in the Monday after and as soon as the ultrasound started, I knew the pregnancy was over. The twins no longer had a heartbeat. To make matters worse it was my birthday. I didn't know how to feel, but I knew this was not the end of the road for me.

After the loss of the twins. I took a break to let my body heal, I switched jobs to a less physically demanding job to allow my body to be relaxed and ready.

I scheduled another transfer; the transfer was confirmed to be a success. I again, went in every two days for blood work and ultrasound. The baby was healthy, growing and then at sixteen weeks, I graduated from my specialist to a high-risk doctor to see me through the rest of the pregnancy.

I did not make it for the full 40 weeks. I went into labor early at twenty-three weeks, but I am happy to announce I have a SON. He is now six years old and healthy. I truly believe it was a combination of me needing to change my mindset along with God's timing that led to me receiving my blessing. All you need is faith the size of a mustard seed and God will see you through. Be on the lookout for the rest of my journey and my experience as a NICU mom.

The Loss of A Child

The Loss of A Child

Chapter Three

Angels in the Skies

Madam Jai Qui

The Loss of A Child

Madam Jai Qui is the owner of Sassy Q's Waist Beads & Accessories and a Bedroom Kandi consultant. Madam's daily affirmation sounds a little like this, "I release any negativity attached to me as I humbly embrace my new beginnings with open arms, a clear mindset and a 20/20 vision in alignment with the universe." This past September, Madam published her very first book, "*A Taste of Madam's Frequencies*" which can be found on Amazon. It consists of relatable poems that walk you through her journey to tranquility. .

She aspires to live a stress-free life surrounded with genuine love to push her to keep going. Stability for her two sons & herself. Madam's name will ring bells in rooms that she has never thought she would walk into. Madam is a wounded healer. Helping others heal while striving to be healthier mentally, spiritually, physically & emotionally gives her purpose. Madam has been on her healing journey for a few years now. "*Poetry saved my life.*" Looking for a healthy outlet for healing & daily self-care was starting to get the best of her. She turned to poetry for a release and hasn't looked back.

Angels in the Skies

As a little girl and even as a grown woman, I have yet to learn how to jump rope (well Double Dutch to be specific.) Back then, playing softball with the boys was more of my thing. In my mind I was a lil tomboy and there were stipulations whenever we played softball.

It was summertime in the Chi, hot as ever outside and I wasn't a skinny girl (never have been.) With that being said, they already knew that unless I hit a homerun, I was not doing no running to first, second, third or home base. Which meant that one of them had to do the running for me because my sassy tail was going to take my time walking to each base. This behavior would only slow the game down, but I did not care.

There was this cute guy that would be out there playing with us. He was so fine and had the most adorable birthmark on his neck. He stayed right down the street from me, and Lord knows that I had the biggest crush on him. Baby, running those bases was the last thing on my mind. I was too cute to risk falling and dirtying up my clothes in front of him. No thank you! Outside of softball, when we were younger, we played Red Light Green Light, "It", Catch a Girl Kiss a Girl, Rock Teacher, Blind Man's Bluff and my favorite game, "House." Of course, I was the mama and my "lil friend" was the daddy.

We had a "love child" that I did not bother telling him about. All that mattered was that I knew, and my friends did too. I just didn't want my "baby daddy" to think that I was crazy and besides, we were too young to live together as a family anyway. So that was that... Oh and speaking of babies. There was this good ole pregnancy pact. How could I ever forget about it? We had it all planned out too. I'm talking 'bout from the sex of our babies on down to their names, our future husbands and our dream homes that we planned to live happily ever after in.

Although my life has not panned out the way that I thought it would, I have no regrets. From experience, I have learned that time does not wait for anyone. I am still learning to be present and enjoy each moment as they come. The years have passed on by and it is quite interesting seeing how my life has taken a turn.

As much as I wish this day had never happened, sadly it did and the only way I will continue to truly heal from my past trauma is to share my testimony. So here we go…

Ten plus years ago, my boyfriend (at the time) and I were in Blockbuster (the one that was next door to Popeyes) right there on Cermak & Cicero (on the west side of Chicago). We had a date night planned. Netflix & chill was not a thing back then, we just called it a movie night. So, I was searching for a couple of movies for us to watch while Bae was looking for a game system and a few games to purchase. All of a sudden, I started feeling sharp pains in my abdominal area, and honestly my tolerance for any amount of pain is very low. Knowing that I can be over the top at times, I tried to stay calm and breathe through the cramps. Reassuring myself that this is an every month thing & the cramps would pass, but this pain felt different. My gut was telling me that something was not right. I went to find Bae to let him know what was going on and we left immediately. Empty handed and all, movie night was canceled. We left the store, we hopped on the bus, Bae made sure I got home safely and then we went our separate ways. I took a shower, popped a Midol and got in the bed with my heating pad with high hopes of sleeping the pain away.

Earlier that next morning, I woke up and was still in excruciating pain. My heating pad served me no justice and honestly it was like I never took a pain pill. The house was quiet as a mouse when I woke up. That only meant one thing, everyone was still asleep. I was not trying to wake anyone up, so I decided to tiptoe out of my bedroom and make my way to the bathroom. The moment I sat down on the toilet, I felt big blood clots dropping into the toilet. Right away, I knew this wasn't normal. Out of curiosity, I looked at the clots and noticed one was the shape of a baby's head. Crushed and afraid is what I felt in that moment. My mama was in her room, but I was afraid to tell her. I did not want her in my business. Thinking to myself, she's going to judge because she does not understand what it feels like to be my age. She never experienced anything like this. Silly right? I know but I was in a panic state of mind.

I had never experienced a pregnancy, let alone a miscarriage. Although I knew what I saw, I tried not to get too worked up, but I just could not ignore the fact that I did not feel like myself. I knew something was not right with my body. It was still a little early and the doctor's office was not open yet. I had to wait a few more hours to call my doctor. Hoping that a same day appointment would be open. When I did call, thankfully, they were able to squeeze me in. The doctor and I had a brief conversation about my symptoms. I also had to take a pregnancy test and have blood work done. I tried to stay positive when I was speaking to the doctor, but positivity went out the window when I was delivered with bad news. The pregnancy test came back positive but based on the symptoms I was experiencing, a miscarriage.

Pregnant with my first child, being informed that I was miscarrying, not having answers as to why this was happening to me just didn't sit well with my spirit. I was angry, disappointed, hurt and I felt like less of a woman. Why me God? Just why me? I had to say goodbye to my unborn child while coming to terms with the fact that I will never be able to hold him, give him penguin kisses, hear his laughter or his cries. I mean that news really broke me. Why God? Why me? I did not ask for this child. How could you take him from me? So many more questions I asked. Hoping for an answer but nothing…

To make matters worse, my family and I were going on vacation to Lake Geneva, I just knew I was not going to be able to enjoy myself. While on vacation, most of my time was spent balled up on the bathroom floor, bleeding & in excruciating pain? I thought menstrual cramps were the devil, but they don't come packing the power that a miscarriage brings. Emotionally I was not in a good place. I felt alone and did not have the courage to tell my mama. She did come to check on me a few times. I just kept telling her I was cramping really bad. I barely ate, slept when I could and when the day came to leave to go back home, I was the first to hop in my daddy's van. We traveled back home with possession of fresh memories, and I continued to keep my secret to myself.

A couple of years went by, and I was welcomed into motherhood. I gave birth to a healthy baby boy. Thankfully there were no complications. I was informed that he had eighty percent hearing loss in his right ear but to this day, you cannot tell by looking at him. He's soaring in school and just recently joined the debate. In one more year, I will have a high schooler and I am proud to call him my son. He's everything that I prayed for.

A few more years had gone by, and motherhood chose me again. I was early on in my pregnancy just as I was when I found out I was expecting my first two unborn babies. I just knew this pregnancy was going to be different. I prayed for a better outcome. I was early on in my first trimester and was already starting to show. Jesus take the wheel! I was going to be huge, and I knew it. I kept telling my family that this baby was going to be a girl or twins. Twins ran on both of our dad's side of the family. I made a promise to myself that I was going to enjoy this pregnancy and there will be no stressing allowed. I was going to be better prepared this time around.

Well, at least I thought I was. Within weeks, I started experiencing minor cramps but not much bleeding. So, I went to the doctor for a checkup, they advised me that I was at risk of losing my baby. I was in tears, thinking to myself, "Not again!" The doctor told me to go home, get some rest, stay off my feet as much as possible and not to stress. That was easier said than done. I was newly engaged and in the midst of planning a wedding, on top of being pregnant. Planning our wedding was my biggest stressor, until my mama took the majority of my worry away so I could focus on carrying our baby to full term. Please do not get me started on everyday life in general. Within a week of finding out I was expecting another bundle of joy, I ended up miscarrying yet again. I went to the doctor just to confirm what I already knew. This was not my first rodeo.

Being told by my doctors that they still have no answers as to why I miscarried for the second time worried me even more, but I trust God. I know that He makes no mistakes, I did not question Him this time around, but I was extremely emotional. I felt like a failure. Our family was excited about this baby. I really wanted this for us. God on the other hand had His own plans. I cried and pleaded with Him for understanding. I heard the words, "Be patient" and that was good enough for me. This miscarriage was painless, and I give thanks for that. I allowed my family to console me, and we carried on with our lives knowing that everything happens in divine timing.

The following year, I found out that I was pregnant again and this little one was causing problems from the womb. When I was pregnant with him, I bled a little bit, and I did not hesitate to get myself checked out. My mom and I went to the emergency room. They did an ultrasound and believe it or not, the little stinker looked right into the camera, he started smiling and was waving at us. Meanwhile I was in pain and worried that I was about to lose another child. Nevertheless, I was relieved to hear his heartbeat, grateful to see that he was healthy and fine. Can I just say that he's still causing problems here on earth? Giving me a run for my money. He is such a sweet kid. My gentle giant. I love him to death, and I would not have things any other way.

A piece of my heart healed each time I gave birth to my sons, but I will never forget about their siblings. There is not a day that goes by that I do not think about them. I pray that our angels continue to watch over mommy & their brothers. I know that the Man above makes no mistakes and each day I pray that He continues to give me peace, strength and understanding. I also give thanks to the two boys who chose me as their mom. I cherish the moments that I'm blessed to spend with them. I strive each day to become a better version of the woman I was yesterday. I will continue to walk in my truth. I share my story in hopes that it reaches other moms who can relate. They need to know that they are not alone. We got this!

Mommy's Little Angels

When the test results confirmed what my womb already knew, never in a million years did I imagine living the rest of my life without you two. My heart aches at the thought of never being able to experience the joys of hearing y'all heartbeats, unlimited penguin kisses, tickling those tiny feet & witnessing each of those memorable milestones. Our family was just as excited about meeting you all as I was. Sadly, that day never came. I've failed y'all & the family too. Mommy is so sorry that I didn't have the power to save you two. There isn't a day that goes by that I don't think about how different my life would be if y'all were here. I often dream about who you all would've looked like. I bet

53

those smiles would brighten my darkest days. There's peace in my heart knowing that I was blessed to carry you two even if for a short while my child. Behave yourself up there. Tell NaNa & Granddaddy that mommy misses them so much. I love you guys forever & always!!

The Loss of A Child

The Loss of A Child

Chapter Four

When the Promise is Deferred, but Not Denied!

Lisa Seymour

Lisa Seymour, serves as an Associate Minister at Logan Street Baptist Church under the leadership of her husband, Pastor David J. Seymour. Lisa, is the Founder of Broken 2 Be Blessed Ministries, LLC and released her first book, "*After The Fall*", last year and a updated version this February.

Lisa Seymour, is a Spiritual Midwife, Author, Speaker, and Teacher. Lisa continues her passion to serve and spread the Gospel through her role as Program Director for a Private Child Welfare Service Agency. Lisa, knows that she has been called to extend grace and mercy, and speak life to those whom the world has deemed as unfit to be used for great things in the kingdom. Lisa holds a M.Div with an emphasis in Pastoral Care from Northern Seminary.

Lisa lives in Dekalb, IL with her husband and their amazing son, David Christian.

When the Promise is Deferred, but Not Denied!

How many times have God revealed a thing to you, but because of your current life challenges you don't see how or when it shall come to pass? That was the story of my journey to motherhood until the day the Promise that I once thought was denied had only been deferred and I gave birth to our son.

My journey to motherhood often takes me back to the book of Genesis, where and the story of Abraham and Sarah. Many of us are familiar with the story of Abraham and Sarah, who before the Promise to be the parents of many nations, were known as Abram and Sarai. When God began to speak to Abram, now Abraham, about the Promise, Abraham could not see how it would be done because Sarah and Abraham were advanced in age. Isn't that just like us to doubt what God has said based on what we see? When we can't see how a thing will work out, we begin to allow doubt and fear to creep in and we think that we are being denied the promise, when the promise is just being deferred. This would be a lesson I would learn as I went on ten-year journey to motherhood.

Growing up I had my life planned out because I saw my mother have my twin sisters at the age of 35. Watching my parents raise teenagers in their 50's, was never a part of my plan. My plan was to get married by the age of 25, have my first child, and be done having children by the age of 27. God must have gotten a kick out of my plan and although I had much heartache on this journey, it taught me many valuable lessons that I pray will encourage you to trust, that although your promise appears to be denied, don't give up, it is just deferred.

Some would say that a young lady in her twenties should be having the time of her life. Believe me I did, but nothing would prepare me for what my twenties would teach me. These would become the years that everything my parents taught me, as well as the things that I had learned in church, would become real.

The summer before my 22nd birthday, I found out that I was pregnant. My pregnancy was going well, I had the support of my family, and friends. I remember it like it was yesterday, a call from the doctor came explaining to me that I needed to have a more invasive ultrasound because my child's spinal cord did not look like it was developing properly; they believed that my child had Spina Bifida, and if that was the case a decision had to be made to keep the pregnancy or terminate. How was I supposed to make that type of decision? No, my pregnancy was not the way I planned, but it was my saving grace. I went to my appointment, the results came back that my child was fine, and a boy.

My third oldest sister met me there and I was able to share in the excitement of learning that my baby boy was healthy! I started to shop and prepare for his delivery. Then about three weeks after finding out my son was healthy and the pregnancy was going well, my life was shattered! I woke up in the early morning of October 1, 1999, to very sharp back pains. I thought it was because I had been on my feet all day and a hot bath would soothe me. The hot bath was not the answer. The pain started to get worse and coming back-to-back. I called out to my roommate and told her that I needed to go to the hospital. About 15 minutes later, I was in the ambulance heading to the hospital with hopes that the doctors would help me, and my pregnancy would continue.

Well, it was at this time that I learned what a mother's love really was. I was twenty-four weeks at this time, the doctor who was attending to me shared that there was internal bleeding and they needed to start me on antibiotics to give my son and I a fighting chance. All I can remember was saying God , "If you have to take one of us, take me. My thinking was that I had fallen so far out of grace with God that my son deserved the chance to fulfill his God-ordained purpose and live.

The antibiotics were administered and attempts to stop labor, but nothing was working. With worry in his eyes the doctor said, "Lisa, we have to prepare to deliver." I said "no, it's too soon." The doctor's response was, "at this point this is the only way to give you both a fighting chance." All of my upbringing and Sunday School teachings came back to my remembrance, and the name of Jesus began to flow from my mouth. I chose to have a c-section because my family was not there. I was ready for the labor pains to be over, and be done. Surrounded by friends, I was prepped to go into surgery trusting that all would be well.

My son, who had been named Stephen Xavier, was flown to a hospital that was more equipped to care for premature babies. Due to my condition, I had to stay back. My son's father went to the hospital to be with Stephen Xavier, and I continued to pray that God would perform a miracle. After everyone had begun to go home, I gave myself a few shots of morphine, so I thought, and dozed off to sleep hoping that God would answer my prayer to take me.

While sleeping, the song by Hezekiah Walker, "Second Chance", wrang loudly in my ear. It was at this moment that I knew what the outcome would be. While sitting talking with another sister who had come to be with me, we received a call from my son's father that our son, Stephen Xavier, did not make it. All I could do was throw the phone and ask why? My sister called for the nurse, they attempted to console me, but nothing could make the pain of losing my son go away. So many questions went through my mind. How did the doctors not see the internal bleeding only a few weeks prior? What did I do wrong? Why did God choose to save me and not my innocent son?

Then my doctor came in and shared words with my sister and I that would change my life forever, "Lisa, based on the test we have run on your son and you, you will never have children." It felt like the wind was just knocked out of me. Here I was, 22 years old, and was just told after losing my son that I would never be able to have children. Anger sat in and the last thing I wanted to hear was God was with me. Being discharged from the hospital without Stephen Xavier was rough, but my village covered me.

Looking back, I needed to start therapy. Here was a 22-year-old young woman who was told that she would never have children, which went against all that she had grown to understand was her role. Go to college, graduate, get a good job, get married, and start a family. What was to become of me if I could not live up to those expectations? My depression was real, but like always I masked how I truly felt and kept going on with life as if losing my son never happened. I found myself longing to feel my son moving inside of me and I was willing to do whatever it took to get that feeling back. From becoming promiscuous to drinking excessively, I longed to get that feeling back. I would go on to lose a series of pregnancies which made me feel the doctors were correct.

Fast forward six years, I was in a much better spiritual, mental, and emotional space. God blessed me with my husband, Dr. David Seymour, and I knew things would be different. I thought that because I was now in an authentic relationship with God, getting married, and starting to walk in purpose, surely God would bless my womb. I began to pray and had dreams of having a baby. I asked God not to take out my mistakes on my husband and in a calm still voice, I heard God say, "It's going to happen!" I began to work-out and eat better, thinking that was the answer. Shortly after we married, we found out we were pregnant. Excited and scared at the same time, I told my husband; because of my history we immediately called the doctor to be seen as soon as possible.

We were able to get an appointment the following week, and our world was shattered by what the we would see. Based on the information that I had given the doctor, I should have measured 5 weeks but the ultrasound was empty. The look of disappointment in my husband's face while still trying to be supportive, broke me. The doctor tried to give us the reason for what could have happened and summed it up to be a blighted ovum. I remembered what God said and I would not take what the doctor was saying as my reality. The doctor scheduled me for a follow-up a few weeks out, we left the doctor's office.

On the way home I kept saying in my head, God, you told me it was going to happen, now I need you to show up. Even though I was standing strong on what God told me, I would be telling a lie if I didn't say that I did not waver in my faith. I had to keep repeating, "Lord, I do believe, but help my unbelief" (Mark 9:24, NLT).

The weeks seemed to go by slowly, but finally our appointment had come, and we went in for our ultrasound. The ultrasound was for a routine checkup, hoping everything was returning to normal. To our surprise there was an embryo and sac. My husband and I both looked at each other with the biggest smiles and the doctor turned to me and said, "*You had to have your dates off because that's a baby and there is a heartbeat.*" My response to her was no, I just went to see the chief Doctor after the last visit, and He showed up. My husband and I left the appointment and went to celebrate. My pregnancy began to progress well, and our child was growing. I continued to speak what I had been promised then one evening after returning from work, our life was shattered again.

I felt a certain urge to go to the bathroom and it was evident that something was wrong, and all I could do was scream, "Not again!" My husband came running and when he saw the evidence, he rushed me to the hospital. It took the staff a long time to get us checked in and we began to demand to be seen immediately. After they heard the tone of my husband's voice, the nurse came and took us back. We get to our room; the doctor came into the room and had no bedside manners. He said, *"Looks like another loss."* From that moment forward we requested that he no longer cares for me, and another doctor be assigned. Sitting there I started thinking like Sarah, how could I give my husband the child we were promised.

I was 30 years old and according to society my biological clock was ticking. After having to deliver our son, John, at 4 months I turned to my husband and asked him *"how could you love me when I can't even give you a child?"* He took me by the hand and said because through thick and thin, we are in this together. Then he held me in his arms. That was when I knew that no matter what we go through we will make it.

We returned to our home only to find evidence of what we had just experienced and all I could do was just fall to the floor wailing. My husband picked me up and put me in the bed, and I stayed there for the next couple of days. On the third day, I woke up and although we were in the fall season the *"Son"* was shining bright through our bedroom window. I got up, took a shower, did my hair, put on some clothes, and went out. The stares of those who knew what had just happened were piercing, but I pressed through the day to enjoy getting back to some normalcy. My husband and I decided that we would take some time away from trying to build our family, but I still felt inadequate because I couldn't have a baby and thought I was worthless.

All while I was going through these different emotions, I continued to hear God say, "It's going to happen!" It was at this moment that I understood how Abraham and Sarah must have felt when God told them they were going to have a son, but based on what they saw and their age, they doubted. I believe even though there was some doubt and even manipulation on the part of Sarah's part giving Hagar to Abraham, God allowed the Promise to be Deferred but not Denied.

Nine months after the loss of John, I came home for my lunch break, and something told me to take a pregnancy test. I said, "Girl, why would you do that? You know you are not pregnant." Well, I did and to my surprise the test was positive. I started screaming and immediately called my husband, "*I said, "Bae, you're going to be a daddy!*" He said, "*Stop playing.*" I said, "*I am not, the test says, pregnant.*" He said, "*I am on my way.*" He came home and I handed him the test, and we both just started smiling and thanking God.

Again, we got on the phone to schedule a doctor's appointment as soon as we could. We were able to get in the next week, when we walked into our appointment, we were seen by one of the interns. At first, I got upset, but to our surprise she was our blessing. She came into the room, reviewed my chart, and said "*I am not going to touch you until we find out why you have had so many losses.*" She continued to say, "*I am going to write you a referral to be seen by both our office and the medical team at Loyola University because we need to find out why you are not going full-term.*" My husband and I asked if she would at least do an ultrasound and she did. We were able to hear our baby's heartbeat. Things were going good, and at each appointment our baby's heartbeat was strong. Even though we had experienced the loss of our son before; this time felt different. We knew that this pregnancy was going to make it.

I went in for my four-month checkup and the doctor looked at me with concern in her eyes, she said *"Lisa, your cervix is thinning."* I said, *"How could that be? It is too early."* She said, *"Based on your history and what I see now, you have an incompetent cervix."* The doctor continued to say that I could go on complete bed rest and see if the cervix would close back up on its own, or I can have a cerclage put in place that would close my cervix, but moderate bed rest would be needed, and it is a 50/50 chance that you can lose your baby. She could tell by the look in my eye that I was about to lose it. She looked at me and said take a minute to call your husband, and your support system so that you can make a decision.

The doctor left the room just as I was about to start crying and yell, *"Not again!"* I heard the Lord say, *"Promised Deferred, not Denied."* Immediately my tears stopped and I called my husband. We discussed our options and elected to have a cerclage. We called our family and intercessors as we prepared for surgery, there was a peace that fell over us. After about four hours, I returned to my room to find my husband waiting, he said *"how do you feel?"* I said *"good."* The doctor came in to check me and said we will watch you overnight to ensure no bleeding or labor, and immediately I said, *"I won't."*

The doctor returned the next morning to check me and was surprised that there was no bleeding. I told her, God made sure that all would be well. She looked at me and said *"yes,*

The Loss of A Child

He did." From that day forward, my doctor visits would increase and I would begin to take shots weekly. Even with all that at 34 weeks our son, David, said he was ready to see the world.

On January 17, 2008 we welcomed our son David Jr. into the world at 5 pounds and 13 ounces. He was the biggest baby in the NICU. We were told he would have to stay until his original due date, but God said not so. David Jr. came home after being in the hospital for about three weeks and we now have a handsome, intelligent, caring, loving, God-fearing 15-year-old young man.

The loss of a child whether during pregnancy or after you have experienced the joy of raising them is never easy, but what I can tell you is that God will be with you through each loss even when you are angry with Him. For those of you, like me, who have experienced lost a child during pregnancy, let me encourage you to not give up because the Promise may be deferred for a moment, but it is not denied.

Get you a good support system, find a therapist to process your emotions with, and most importantly trust God and His process.

The Loss of A Child

The Loss of A Child

Chapter Five

You'll Always be my Angel Baby

Timothia Reid

Educator, book lover, and author ***Timothia Reid*** is passionate about pretty much anything in print and improving the quality of life of children in her community. She has over 10 years of experience in education, where she has worn many hats, such as teacher's aide, substitute teacher, Title 1 aide, and classroom teacher. She has an Associate's degree in Early Childhood Education, a Bachelor's degree in Psychology, and a Master's degree in Education with a concentration in Reading Literacy. Timothia is working on her second Master's degree through Grand Canyon University in Teaching English as a Second Language (TESOL). She is on the Black Advisory Board for Scholastic, where she shares her passion for books by providing teachers and students with resources to improve literacy quality in classrooms.

She is also a speaker on the Art of Transparency Tour, where she shares her story with those who are willing to listen and learn. Timothia currently lives in Illinois, a mother of two adult children which she loves to spend time with in her free time, read books, and enjoy life to the fullest. She has even ventured into acting in plays recently.

You'll Always be my Angel Baby

I will never forget... I remember it like it was yesterday... I wonder every day who you would have become... I wonder if you would have been more like me or more like him... I wonder how you would have fit in with your brother and sister... My sweet Angel baby... I wish I could have held you in my arms and kissed your sweet face... I just keep wishing for things that will never be... I cannot even say, "Until we meet again," because there has not been a first time yet...

I remember the excruciating pain that started as I boarded the plane with my 10-month-old son in January 2001. We were headed back home from Puerto Rico after visiting my parents for Christmas. I was excited to return home to see my husband, who had graciously made this trip a reality. You see, we were in the military then and weren't making much money. Just enough to pay the necessary bills. My husband had been working a second job to help bring in extra money for the house. Paying for daycare for an infant was an expensive necessity with the type of work that we did and the hours we worked. You see, at that moment, it was unbeknown to me that I was pregnant again, even though I had started to notice that I had been sleeping a lot throughout my short trip back to my childhood home. The pain only got worse by the time we landed back in North Carolina, where we lived at the time. I was almost bent over in pain, but I had to push through because I had an infant in my lap for the whole flight, which also had a layover because, at the time, there were no straight flights available.

When we finally arrived and my husband picked us up from the airport, I told him how I had been feeling during the flight. We thought that maybe it was something that I may have eaten, so I decided to take some medicine and lay down with the hope that the pain would subside. The pain only got worse as the hours went by. As a matter of fact, it got so bad that we ended up going to the emergency room because the pain was excruciating. We discovered I was pregnant with our second child during this emergency room visit. You can imagine our shock because this was our second unplanned pregnancy, and we were already struggling financially as it was. Nonetheless, we were still happy. A baby is a blessing from God, and we would do whatever it took to make life comfortable for our babies. We were sent home with this news, and we were beginning to get excited about the whole ordeal. The hospital just dismissed the pain as part of the pregnancy. I don't remember if I was given any medication for the pain, but I know things only worsened after that.

The next night, we returned to the emergency room again because the pain had not subsided. As a matter of fact, the pains were continuously getting worse. It was during this visit that we found out my life was in danger. You see, my baby was stuck in one of my Fallopian tubes. I had to have immediate surgery because a baby growing inside my tube could cost me my life. There was no chance that my baby would survive, but I could. Imagine just being told the day before that you are pregnant and, in less than 24 hours, being told that your pregnancy will kill you. Needless to say, I was rushed into surgery to have my tube and my pregnancy removed. It is called an ectopic pregnancy, and I had never heard of such a thing until that day. I remember being scared to be that close to death once again. It seemed like the devil kept trying to come after me for some reason.

I know that God has a reason for everything, and while I never understood why this happened, I know He knows best. I made it through surgery successfully and was told that due to this ectopic pregnancy and the removal of one of my Fallopian tubes, it would be difficult for me to conceive again. Little did they know that God had other plans!

I was sent home a few days later and put on medical leave for a week to recover. This was one of the worst times of my life, but it had nothing to do with the pregnancy. During this time, I also found out some things about my marriage that no woman ever wants to hear. However, that's a story for another book. I struggled with my emotions about the events that had just transpired. I was happy to be alive and that they had gotten me into surgery when they did because I was apparently very close to not being able to be here to tell you, my story. I was truly saddened by the thought of what could have been.

Throughout the rest of that year, I would reminisce about how far along I would have been and what my baby would have looked like. Would it have been a boy or a girl? Would he/she get along well with his/her brother and sister? I named my baby Angel because it seemed fitting and would accommodate both genders. My sweet *Angel* baby. Through the years, I still wonder what he/she would have become, and I mourn the loss daily. Some days are better than others, but I don't really discuss these feelings with anyone. As a matter of fact, this is the first time I am openly sharing this with anybody.

People may think that losing a child at this very early stage is probably easier than if the child had actually been born. To me, it feels worse because I never got to feel my baby growing inside of me or kicking me. I never got to see their face. I never even got to say goodbye. It was inside me before I went to surgery, and then it was gone when I woke up. Many have said that I should be happy because my life was saved, and Yes, I am grateful. Please understand that I am thankful for being alive. However, I still wonder what could have been and how life would have been different. I wonder what they would have looked like and what kind of personality they would have had. So many questions run through my mind as the tears roll down my face. It is not easy! This feeling of loss will never go away. I will never get my questions answered. I just hope that one day, if or when I make it to Heaven, a little boy or girl will approach me and tell me, "Hi, Mommy! It's me, your Angel baby!" Just that simple thought warms my heart and gives me hope. Unfortunately for you all, I will not be able to share that moment with anyone.

Until we meet, my sweet Angel baby. I cannot wait to hug and kiss you when I finally meet you! Until then, please watch over us and help keep us safe…I love you, my sweet Angel baby.

The Loss of A Child

The Loss of A Child

Conclusion

Thank you for taking the time to purchase and read "The Loss of A Child"

In this anthology, we the Authors, wanted to share our story of Losing a child, we wanted to let you know that you are not alone and we all experience loss in a different way. Allow yourself time to grieve, without feeling guilty about how long it may take. You are the only person that can determine when you are better. We also want you to know that we know and understand that this is one of the hardest traumas to overcome, take your time. Take it one day, one minute, one second at a time…. Please KNOW that you can and will get through this.

For the **BIBLE** says:

- Matthew 5:4 – "Blessed [are] they that mourn: for they shall be comforted."

- 1 John 14:27 – "Peace I leave with you; my peace I give you. I do not give to you as the world gives."

- Psalms 34:18 – "The LORD is nigh unto them that are of a broken heart; and saveth such as be of a contrite spirit."

- Psalms 147:3 – "He healeth the broken in heart, and bindeth up their wounds."

- Psalm 73:26 – "My flesh and my heart may fail, but God is the strength of my heart and my portion forever."

And as I always say…. These are just a few. We must remember that God is a keeper of all things and will never forsake you. Your right now is for somebody else's tomorrow. We stand to help others behind us.

Remember that your prayers are being heard. You must continue to take the time to heal, continue to have faith in knowing that God is working on your behalf.

Thank you!

Invisible Daughter LLC

Under the umbrella of Mikkita Moore LLC

www.mikkitamoore.com

The Loss of A Child

The Loss of A Child

www.ingramcontent.com/pod-product-compliance
Lightning Source LLC
Chambersburg PA
CBHW070009100426
42741CB00012B/3172